YOU CAN DRAW
PUPPIES
& DOGS

By Debby Henwood

Illustrated by Charles Russell

Cover illustration by Estella Lee Hickman

Willowisp Press®

For Sarah and her precious puppy Spitz—D. H.

Published by Willowisp Press, Inc.
401 E. Wilson Bridge Road, Worthington, Ohio 43085

Copyright ©1986 by Willowisp Press, Inc.

Printed in the United States of America

10 9 8 7 6 5 4

ISBN 0-87406-120-2

This book will show you how to do step-by-step pencil drawings of puppies and dogs. Draw the body and head shapes, then add the legs, ears, and tail.

Improve the basic shape step-by-step until it is just the way you like it. Then erase the guidelines and add detail and shading. Have fun drawing your favorite pet.

BEFORE YOU BEGIN

Here are some drawing guidelines you should know before you begin to draw the puppies and dogs shown in this book.

1. *Use a pad of paper or six sheets of paper. This pad or "cushion" gives soft lines and shows texture when shading or making hair patterns. You may want to use tracing paper when you first begin. A kneaded eraser will be helpful to lighten shading marks. Have two soft-lead pencils—one semi-pointed and one with a chiseled edge.*

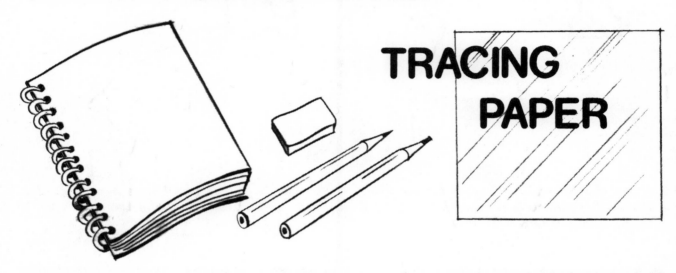

2. *To get a chiseled edge on a pencil use a sandpaper block. Rub the lead back and forth across the sandpaper until the lead on two sides is flat and straight across the edge. Hold the pencil as shown in the illustration.*

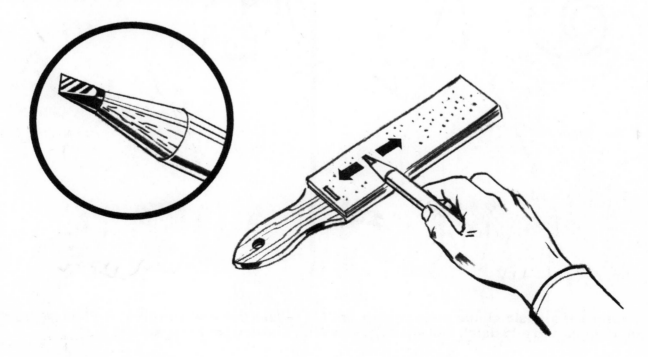

- *To make broad lines over wide areas, lightly press the side of either pencil. The semi-pointed pencil is shown here.*

- *Use the flat edge of the chiseled-edge pencil to make broad strokes. Moving the pencil within your fingers, use the straight edge to make the fine lines. This technique can also be used with the semi-pointed pencil.*

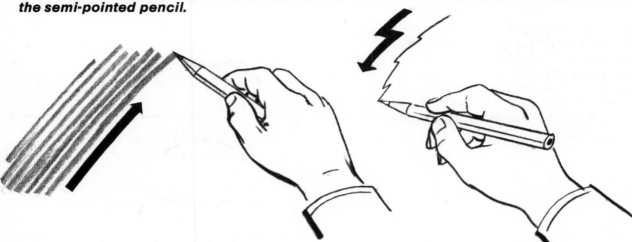

3. *Study the illustrations below for eye placement. Use the eye line and nose line as guides. Notice the different angles of the eyes as the head turns, beginning with the front view to three-quarters view to profile.*

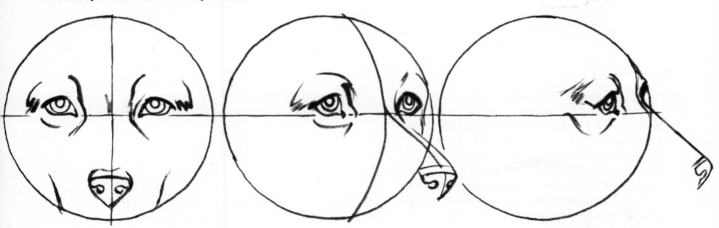

4. *The eyes, ears, and tail add to the character of the breed of dog. Draw these to reflect the mood of the dog. Notice the difference in the body shapes and tails of these dogs.*

DRAWING THE HEAD

1. *This German shepherd's head is turned three-quarters around. Draw the eye and nose lines. Remember that the muzzle is in front of the face. The bridge of the muzzle begins with a line drawn from the center of the face. The end of the nose starts as a square. It is a guide for the mouth.*

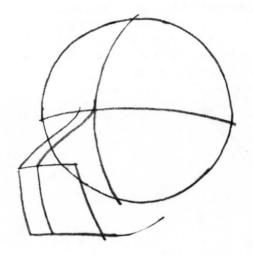

2. *When the dog's head is turned you see more of one side of the face. All ears are placed in the same position on the head, but the shape of the ears are different. These ears stand up and are pointed. A curved line is drawn for the mouth.*

3. Detail is added to the eyes. The hair on the back of the neck is longer than any place else around the head. Remember that hair hides the true structure of the dog.

4. This finished sketch shows a dark muzzle which appears separate from the lighter shaded face. Dark lines along the bridge of the nose, around the eyes, and inside the ears give depth. The dark eye pupils and nose have white spots called "highlights."

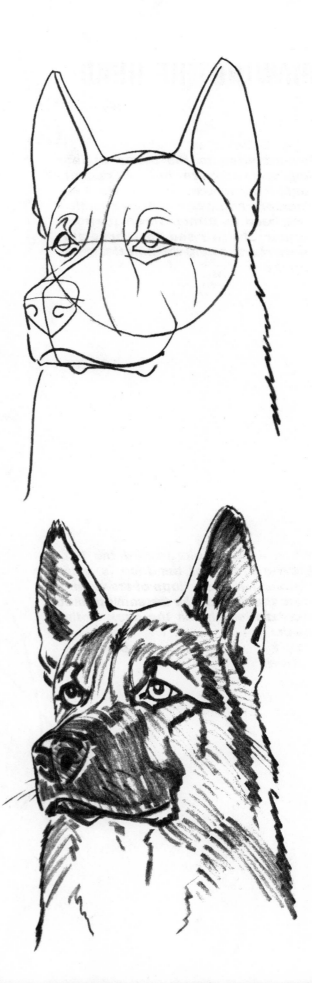

DRAWING THE HEAD

1. *Pay attention to the breed of the dog you are drawing. A cocker spaniel is smaller than a German shepherd and has a shorter muzzle. This head is turned three-quarters around. The eye and nose lines are guides for drawing the muzzle.*

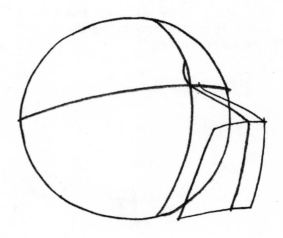

2. *When a dog looks toward the left, the right side of the face is most visible. The long, floppy ears extend from the side of the head. Note that the front ear hides the back of the neck.*

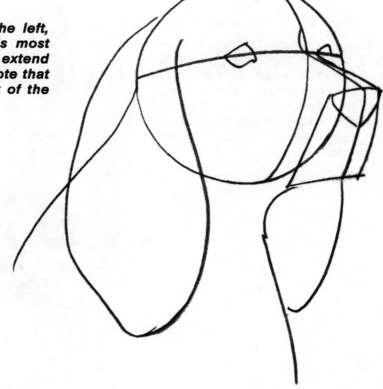

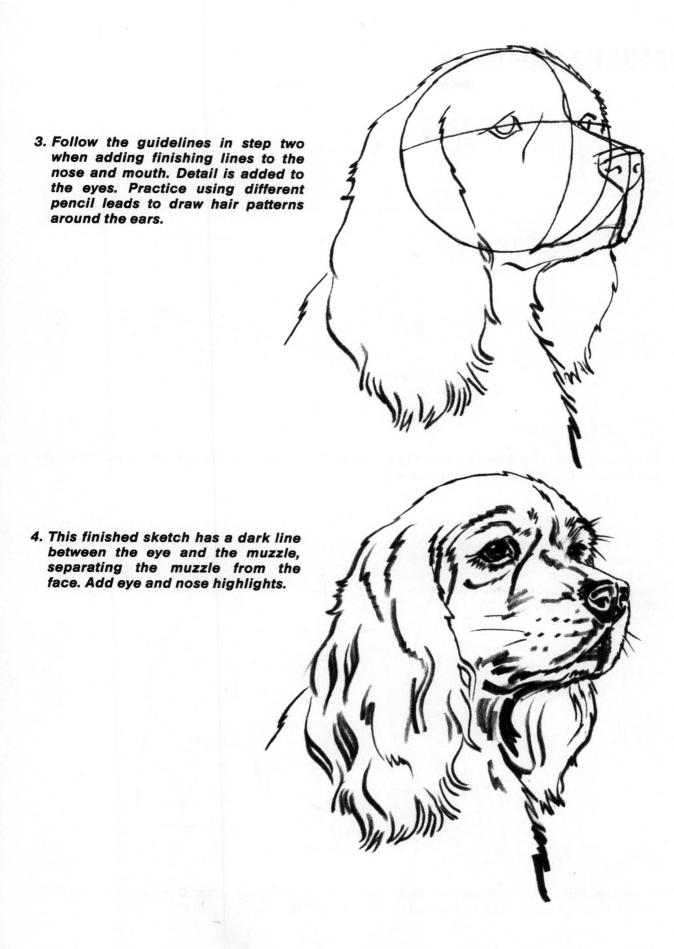

3. Follow the guidelines in step two when adding finishing lines to the nose and mouth. Detail is added to the eyes. Practice using different pencil leads to draw hair patterns around the ears.

4. This finished sketch has a dark line between the eye and the muzzle, separating the muzzle from the face. Add eye and nose highlights.

BASSET HOUND

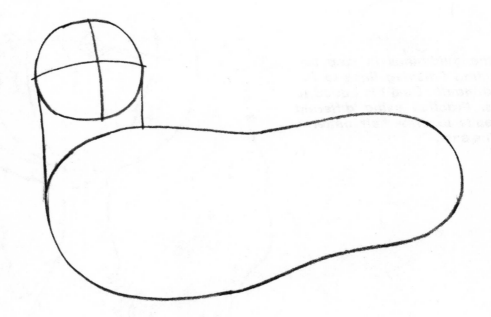

1. This dog is low and long-bodied. Lightly draw the head with the eye and nose lines, then the kidney-shaped body and the neck.

2. Draw the muzzle guidelines and nose on the face. Add long ears. Curved lines are drawn where the legs are joined to the body. Add a long tail.

3. Bassets have sad-looking eyes. Draw the eyeball so only half of it shows. Begin to shape the nose and mouth. Add detail lines to the legs and feet.

4. Erase guidelines. Darken the outline. Draw detail lines. Use broad shading strokes to show hair markings.

BEAGLE PUPPY

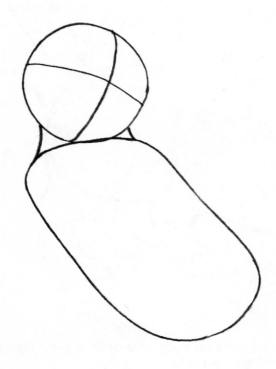

1. *This puppy is a popular pet and hunting dog. Lightly draw a kidney shape for the body. Draw the head tilted to the side.*

2. *Draw lines on the face for the muzzle and nose. Draw leg shapes. Add floppy ears.*

3. Add features to the face and detail lines. Add the tail.

4. Erase guidelines. Darken the outline around the body. Add more detail lines and eye highlights. Shade in hair markings.

BOXER PUPPY

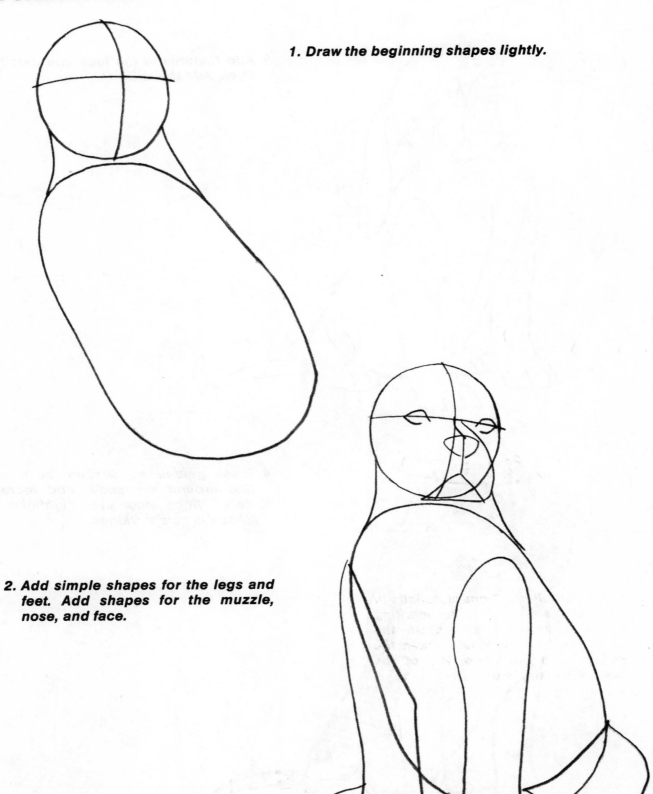

1. Draw the beginning shapes lightly.

2. Add simple shapes for the legs and feet. Add shapes for the muzzle, nose, and face.

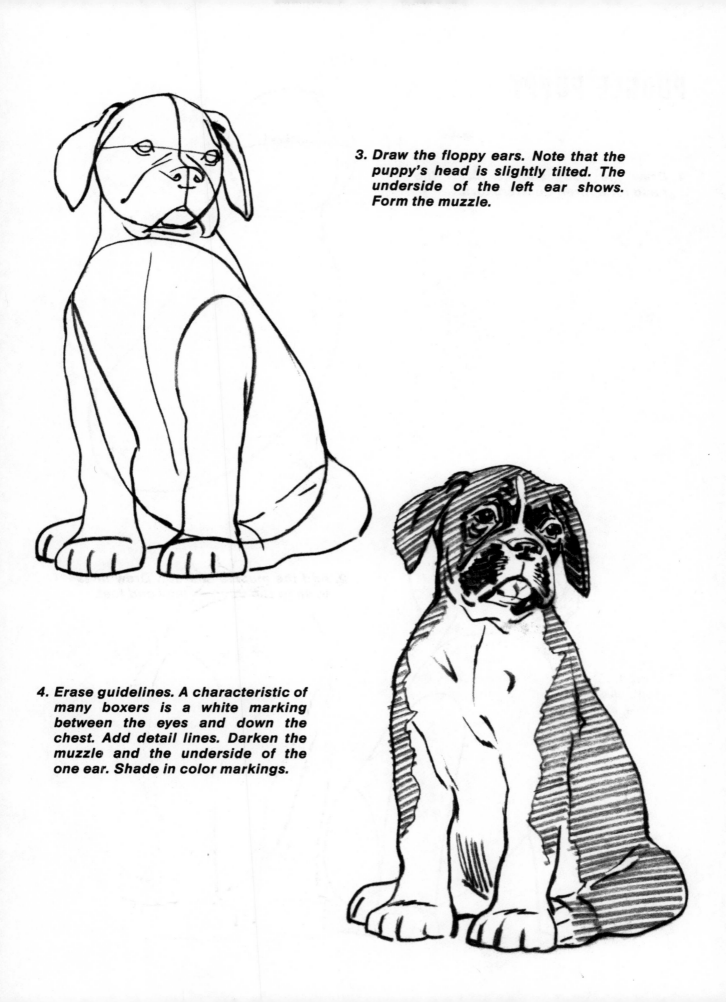

3. Draw the floppy ears. Note that the puppy's head is slightly tilted. The underside of the left ear shows. Form the muzzle.

4. Erase guidelines. A characteristic of many boxers is a white marking between the eyes and down the chest. Add detail lines. Darken the muzzle and the underside of the one ear. Shade in color markings.

POODLE PUPPY

1. Draw the body shapes. Draw the head for a three-quarters turn.

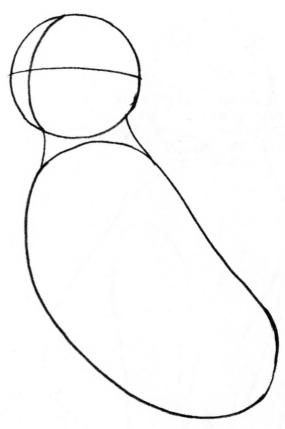

2. Add the muzzle and ear. Draw lines to show the puppy's legs and feet.

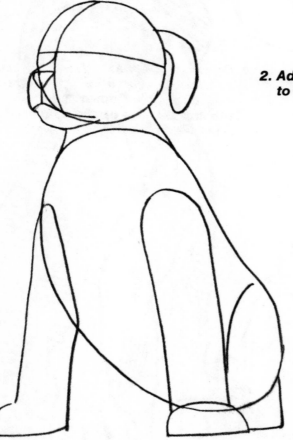

3. Draw a zigzag line for the hair around the basic shapes, adding the tail. Draw the eyes and mouth. Draw a circle for a ball.

4. Erase guidelines. Use the basic shapes as guides for hair patterns. Add curly lines down the chest, on the muzzle, and up the bridge of the nose. Add a design to the ball.

DALMATIAN PUPPY

1. This playful puppy is in a jumping
   position. Draw the beginning shapes.

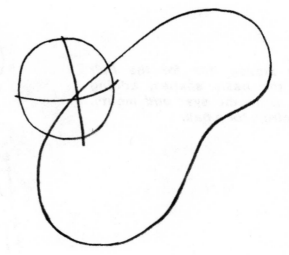

2. Draw the square muzzle and nose.
   When a puppy jumps, the ears flop
   off the face. Draw the ears. Draw
   shapes for the legs. Note that the
   front right foot is touching the
   ground. The other feet are in the air.

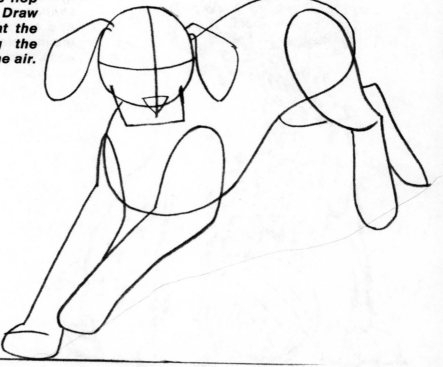

3. Add the eyes, mouth, tongue, and tail.

4. Erase guidelines. Darken the outline. Add detail lines and shading under the ears. Use the side of a pencil to make spots. Add highlights to the eyes and nose.

WEST HIGHLAND WHITE TERRIER PUPPY

1. This popular terrier is a friendly puppy. The head is held high. Draw the basic shapes, slightly tilting the head.

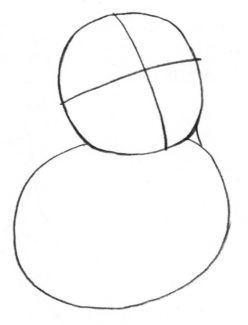

2. The muzzle looks like a ball of fluff. Draw an oval, and then add the nose. Draw shapes for the legs and feet. Add pointed ears and a carrot-shaped tail.

3. **Draw a dark zigzag line around the body. Position the eyes wide apart, then draw the mouth. Draw a ball under the paw.**

4. **Erase guidelines. Follow the basic shapes to shade hair patterns along the legs, down the chest, and from the nose. Highlight the eyes and nose.**

IRISH SETTER

1. This drawing is a profile. Combine the basic shapes for the body.

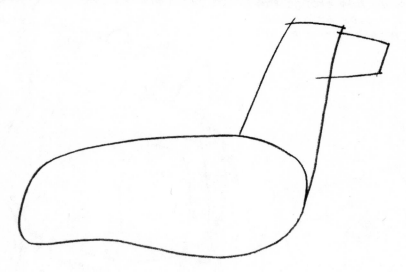

**2. Add feet and leg shapes. Add an ear.
Draw the thin tail at "point."**

3. Draw a dark outline around the dog's body. Note that the hair is "feathered" on the legs. The tail has "fringe." Add wavy lines to the ear. Draw features on the face.

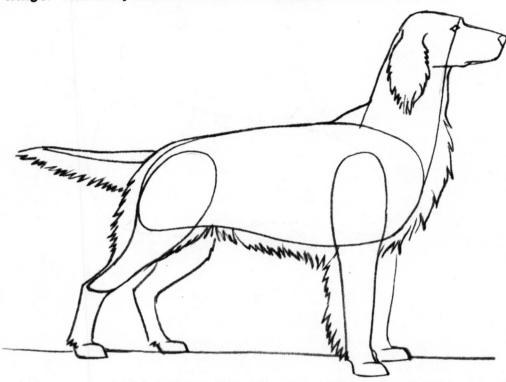

4. Add detail to the face. Shade hair patterns.

GERMAN SHEPHERD

1. Draw the basic shapes for this large, powerful dog.

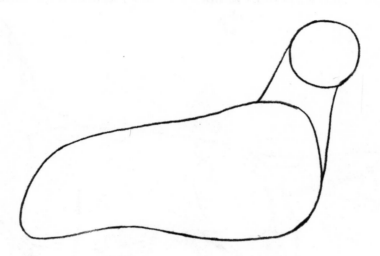

2. Draw the shape for the muzzle. Draw the ears and tail. Add leg and feet shapes.

3. Draw a zigzag outline on the chest, legs, and tail. Draw the eye and nose. Add detail to the ear and mouth.

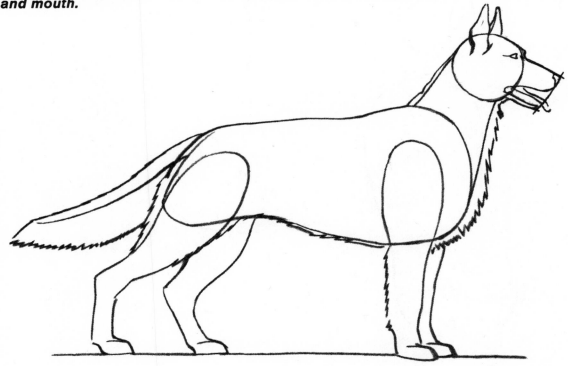

4. Erase guidelines. Darken the outline of the dog. Shade the dog for dark and light color markings.

COCKER SPANIEL

1. This cocker spaniel is begging. Draw the body shapes.

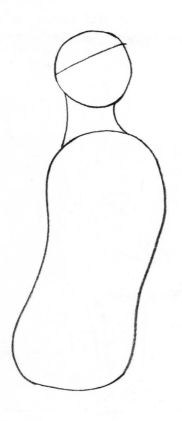

2. Draw the muzzle on the face and the floppy ears. Draw the legs.

3. Draw a wavy outline around the ear, the chest, and the legs to show long hair. Add features to the face. Add a tail.

4. Erase guidelines. Finish the face. Darken the outline. Add detail lines.

COLLIE

1. *This collie is in a running position. It has a long, lean head with a flat skull and a broad neck. Draw the basic shapes.*

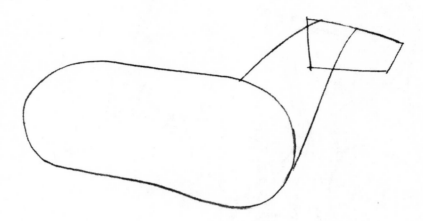

2. *Draw the legs so that the dog's weight is on the front right foot. The other legs are bent and off the ground.*

3. Add features to the face. Draw a zigzag outline to show the hair flowing as the dog runs. Draw the ears angled toward the back of the head.

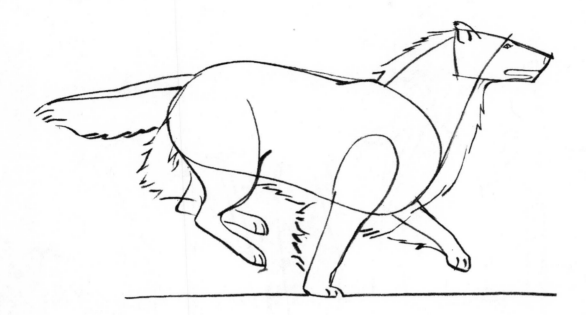

4. Erase guidelines. Add detail. Shade the hair patterns. The mane around the neck is white.

MINIATURE SCHNAUZER

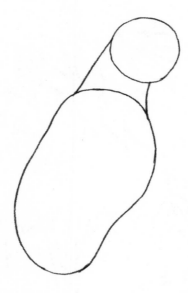

1. *This dog is in a sitting position. Draw the basic shapes.*

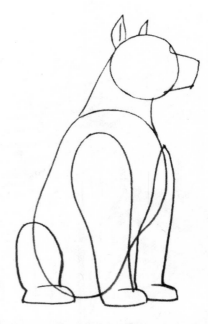

2. *Draw leg shapes. Add shapes for the muzzle and the short, stand-up ears.*

3. *Draw an outline around the dog. The head profile shows a flat forehead, bushy eyebrows, and a beard around the mouth.*

4. *Add detail lines to the face, the chest, and the legs. These areas are usually white. Shade the side of the face and the back.*